Life in Victorian Britain

Brian Williams

Raintree

www.raintreepublishers.co.uk
Visit our website to find out
more information about
Raintree books.

To order:
☎ Phone 0845 6044371
🖹 Fax +44 (0) 1865 312263
🖳 Email myorders@raintreepublishers.co.uk

Customers from outside the UK please telephone +44 1865 312262

Raintree is an imprint of Capstone Global Library
Limited, a company incorporated in England and Wales having
its registered office at 7 Pilgrim Street, London, EC4V 6LB
- Registered company number: 6695582

Edited by Kate de Villiers and Laura Knowles
Designed by Steve Mead and Debbie Oatley
Original illustrations © Capstone Global Library Limited 2010
Picture research by Mica Brancic and Elaine Willis
Production by Alison Parsons
Originated by Chroma Graphics (Overseas) Pte. Ltd
Printed and bound in China by Leo Paper Products Ltd

ISBN 978 0 431193 64 9 (hardback)
14 13 12 11 10
10 9 8 7 6 5 4 3 2 1

ISBN 978 0 431193 71 7 (paperback)
15 14 13 12 11 10
10 9 8 7 6 5 4 3 2 1

British Library Cataloguing in Publication Data
Williams, Brian, 1943-
Life in Victorian Britain. -- (Unlocking history)
941'.081-dc22
A full catalogue record for this book is available from the
British Library.

Acknowledgements

We would like to thank the following for permission to
reproduce photographs: © 2000 Topham Picturepoint
p. **19**; akg-images pp. **6**, **7**; Corbis pp. **22** (© The Francis Frith
Collection), **24** (© Historical Picture Archive); Getty Images
pp. **4** (Roger Fenton), **14** (Hulton Archive), **16** (Otto Herschan/
Oscar Gustav Rejlander), **17** (Paul Martin); Mary Evans
Picture Library pp. **26** (© Illustrated London News Ltd), **28**;
© Mary Evans Picture Library 2008 pp. **9**, **10–11**, **13**, **23**; The
Bridgeman Art Library p. **21**.

Cover photograph of a London 'Knifeboard' omnibus, c. 1865,
London, England, reproduced with permission of Corbis/
Hulton-Deutch Collection.

We would like to thank Bill Marriott for his invaluable help in
the preparation of this book.

Every effort has been made to contact copyright holders of
material reproduced in this book. Any omissions will be
rectified in subsequent printings if notice is given to the
publishers.

All the Internet addresses (URLs) given in this book were valid
at the time of going to press. However, due to the dynamic
nature of the Internet, some addresses may have changed, or
sites may have changed or ceased to exist since publication.
While the author and Publishers regret any inconvenience this
may cause readers, no responsibility for any such changes can
be accepted by either the author or the Publishers.

Contents

Some words are shown in **bold**, like this. You can find out what they mean by looking in the glossary.

The Victorian age

The Victorian age is named after Queen Victoria. She became Britain's queen in 1837, when she was 18 years old, and she ruled until 1901. The 1800s were a time of change. Changes brought about by the **Industrial Revolution**, before Victoria was born, affected everyone. Victoria was not just queen of Britain. She was also queen of Australia, New Zealand, Canada, Jamaica, South Africa, and many other lands in the **British Empire**. In 1876, she became Empress of India, too. Britain ruled the biggest empire of all time, British ships controlled the oceans, and British goods were sold all over the world.

◀ Victoria was the first British queen to have her photo taken. Here she is in 1854. Photography brought the "snapshot", to record a moment in history for ever.

The Victorians gave us two marvellous inventions for unlocking history – photography and sound recording. We can look at photos and films of real people, and listen to crackly records of their voices. We can also read their letters, diaries, books, and newspapers. We can still see some Victorian buildings, Victorian machines, and one or two ships, such as *Warrior* at Portsmouth and *Great Britain* at Bristol. These are the kinds of **evidence** that help us to unlock the secrets of life in Victorian Britain.

Great events of the Victorian age

1819   Victoria is born, in London

1830   Britain's first passenger railway is built

1837   Victoria becomes queen

1838   A steamship crosses the Atlantic Ocean for the first time

1840   The first postage stamps go on sale

1861   The American Civil War begins

1879   Electric light is invented in Britain and the United States

1885   The first car is made, in Germany

1901   Queen Victoria dies

Above is a mini-timeline of Victorian times. In this book, "key" boxes (like this one) explain how different sources can unlock history.

A changing world

Britain was the first country to have an **industrial revolution**. Before the Victorian age, most people lived in small towns and villages, and worked at home or on farms. Few people travelled far and no message went faster than a horse could gallop.

In the 1800s, towns grew and grew, as people moved from the countryside to find work in new factories, coal **mines**, iron works, and **textile mills**. Some towns grew into big cities. London was the biggest city in the world.

▼ Here are two city scenes. The picture below was drawn in 1828. The photograph on page 7 was taken in 1900. How many changes you can spot? Have the roads and traffic changed?

Steam trains thundered along the new railways. People sent messages by **electric telegraph** and posted letters. They rode bicycles, and went shopping in department stores. They lit their homes with gas and electricity, instead of burning candles and oil lamps.

A few factory owners got very rich, but most workers were poor. The poorest families lived in overcrowded **slums**. Gradually, things got better. New laws made factories safer, and towns cleaner. The Victorians built roads, railways, water pipes and drains, bridges, parks, public libraries, town halls, and schools. By 1900, Britain looked very different from how it had been in 1800.

This table shows how important coal was as a fuel. Notice how much more was mined in 1900 than in 1800. Can you think of three ways in which the Victorians used coal? (See also page 10.)

Year	Million tonnes
1800	11.2
1830	22.3
1850	49.8
1860	81.3
1870	111.8
1880	148.3
1900	228.6

The railways

In the early 1800s, engineers Richard Trevithick and George Stephenson built **steam engines** that could drive a locomotive on rails. The age of railways had begun.

The first steam train carried passengers in 1830. Trains rushed along at 50 kilometres per hour (30 miles per hour), hissing and puffing steam and smoke. Some passengers were scared because their doctors warned that the human body would probably explode at such high speeds. Member of **Parliament** William Huskisson was knocked down by a train at the opening of the Liverpool and Manchester Railway in September 1830. However, no passenger died from going at a high speed.

Stephenson's Rocket

George Stephenson (1781–1848) built *Rocket*, the locomotive that pulled the first steam train with passengers in 1830. Stephenson never went to school. He started work on a farm as a boy of eight. Later he worked in coal **mines** in Northumberland, and learned to build steam engines. His son Robert (1803–59) built the first railway into London, but was most famous for building bridges.

A web of railways soon criss-crossed Britain. Tracks were built by gangs of workers or navigators (navvies, for short). There were big stations, like St Pancras in London, and lots of little ones at country towns and villages. After 1863, London trains went underground on the Metropolitan line. Railways changed life for everyone. Milk, vegetables, fish, and other foods went by train. Letters and parcels travelled on special mail trains. Office workers took the train to the city from the **suburbs**. Families took day trips by train, and went to the seaside for summer holidays.

St Pancras Station was built in 1868. This busy scene was painted 40 years later.

See how busy Britain's railways were in 1900 compared to 1845. Block charts like this help us to compare information.

Mines and factories

Victorian factories needed **energy** to keep machines working. Most of this energy came from burning coal. Coal was dug from **mines**. The mine owners sold coal to the factories. Mine owners paid the miners low wages.

Most coal miners worked in underground tunnels, using picks and shovels to dig out the coal. Women and children also worked in the mine tunnels. It was cold, dark, wet, dirty, and dangerous. Children as young as eight worked below ground for 18 hours a day. People known as **reformers** knew this was wrong. They changed things, by making new laws to protect children (see box on page 11).

Dangers of working in a mine

Mining was a very dangerous job. A miner could get hurt or even killed in a number of different ways:

- Falling down the mine shaft (the deep hole from the surface)
- Getting trapped when the shaft is blocked, with no way out
- Breathing in poison gas
- A candle or match could set off a gas explosion
- The mine tunnel, held up by wooden "pit props", could collapse
- Water could flood the mine.

Workers in factories, such as **textile mills**, also had to work hard. A mill girl-worker got up at 5 a.m. She walked to work, and at 5.30 a.m. the machines started working. At 7.30 a.m. she had a break, to clean the machine. At 12 noon she had lunch – perhaps bread and cheese. At 1 p.m. it was back to work, until 7 p.m. when she went home. Many workers had sniffly colds, because mills were warm and damp (to keep the thread strong), and also because dust got in workers' lungs.

New laws

1833	Factory Act stops children under nine from working in factories
1842	No women or children under 10 to work underground in coal mines
1860	No boy miners under 12
1900	No boy miners under 13

▼ "Putters" pushed trucks of coal. "Trappers" opened and shut wooden doors to let air through the tunnels.

Engravings like this help to show us what it was like inside a mine.

Town and country

Britain's population grew from 15 million in 1801 to more than 37 million by 1901. We know this from the **census**, held every 10 years. In 1801, only about 30 per cent of British people lived in towns. About 80 per cent did so by 1901.

In the industrial cities, factory chimneys and steel-making furnaces (heated containers for melting metals such as iron) smoked and glowed day and night. The air was speckled with dust and soot. Rows of small brick houses surrounded the factories, sprawling over what had been green fields.

In the countryside, much of Britain was still fields and woods. There were fewer roads and, until the 1890s, no cars at all. On farms, men, women, and children worked from dawn to dusk. Their work included planting potatoes in spring and cutting corn at **harvest time**. Home was usually a small cottage, often with a garden for vegetables. Poor country children had helthier food and more space to play in than poor city children. By 1881, only one in eight men in Britain worked on farms. Horses still pulled ploughs and carts, but new machines meant farmers did not need so many workers.

Population tables help us compare how fast cities grew during Victorian times. This table shows that many more people lived in London than any other city in Britain. By 1901, London had 6 million people!

City	1801	1851
Leeds	53,000	172,000
Liverpool	82,000	376,000
Manchester	75,000	303,000
Glasgow	77,000	329,000
Birmingham	71,000	133,000
London	1,100,000	2,600,000

Life expectancy

People did not live as long as today. In 1842, a **reformer** published the figures in the table below to show the **average** age when rich and poor people died in town and country. Where were poor people likely to live longest?

	Manchester (town)	Rutland (country)
Poor	17	38
Rich	38	52

This picture shows poor people in the **slums** of Whitechapel, London in about 1870. Pictures like this show how horrible life was for people in city slums.

Home life

At home, much depended on how rich or poor a family was. Sickness and the death of children hit rich and poor alike, but poor families lived in the unhealthiest conditions. The rich had better homes and could afford servants, such as a cook and a nanny for the children. In 1891, the **census** showed there were 2 million house-servants in Britain.

Victorian houses had gas lighting and coal fires to warm the rooms. There was a parlour, which was a special room for visitors. Visitors went to the front door; tradesmen, such as the butcher or someone doing repairs, used the side door. At the top of the house were small rooms for the servants. A bathroom was a luxury. Most people washed at a bedroom washstand using a china basin and jug, in the kitchen, or used an outside pump. Indoor toilets were a luxury, too. Most people had toilets outside called privies, and kept a **chamber pot** under the bed for the night time.

In towns, poor people lived crammed together in small houses with no gardens. Some families shared rooms in **tenement** blocks. Most people paid rent to a landlord – the person who owned the house. Some people had no home of their own, and paid a penny or two for a shared bed in a **lodging house**. The penniless slept in a doorway or under a hedge. Old people, children with no parents, and the jobless were sent to the **workhouse**.

Family finances

This is what part of a family's weekly spending looked like. The figures come from an 1841 book about how the poor lived. This family (two parents, three children) spent about 15s a week on food, rent, heating, and schooling. In Victorian money, s = shilling (5p today), d = penny.

Household bills show us how much people had to spend. You could compare this with what your family buys at the supermarket each week.

Tea, sugar – 1s 6d

Coal – 9d

Potatoes – 1s 4d

Five loaves of bread – 3s 6d

Rent – 2s 6d

School – 4d

Soap and candles – 6d

Victorian families were big. Most children grew up in small, cramped rooms.

Growing up

Victorians had big families. Five children was the **average**, and many couples had 10 or more children. The birth-rate (the number of babies born) reached 34 babies per 1,000 adults in the 1870s. That is three times what it is today. However, many Victorian children died before they were five. Some were underfed, while others caught diseases such as measles.

How children lived depended on whether their parents were very rich (upper class), fairly rich (middle class), fairly poor (working class), or very poor (jobless and homeless). Rich children, with parents who owned a lot of land or a factory perhaps, lived in big houses. They had servants to look after them, went on holidays, and had lots of toys. Middle-class children had a more modest house, with perhaps one servant. Working-class children lived close to the factories, **mines**, or farms where their parents worked. Home was often so crowded that all the children shared one bedroom.

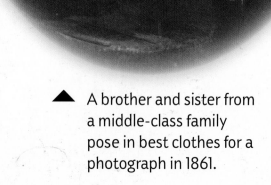

▲ A brother and sister from a middle-class family pose in best clothes for a photograph in 1861.

The poorest children lived on the streets or in the **workhouse**. Many street children slid into crime – like Fagin's gang of pickpockets (street thieves) in Charles Dickens' book *Oliver Twist*. In the 1850s, 14,000 children under 16 were in prison in England, some just for stealing a bottle of ginger beer. In 2008, about 3,000 14- to 17-year-olds were locked up in special children's homes, but we no longer send children to proper prisons.

Dangerous times

Life in Victorian times had lots of dangers for children, such as:

- Working down a coal mine
- Getting your hair tangled or your fingers chopped off by a factory machine
- Sleeping in an alley with only straw to keep you warm
- Going hungry most days
- Being sent to prison for stealing food
- Being hit with a cane at school
- Being run over in a busy street by a horse and cart.

▼ For many children, the street was their playground.

School days

At the start of the Victorian age, not many children went to school, though some parents paid a teacher or child-minder for lessons in reading, writing, and maths. Many boys learned trades such as carpentry. Girls learned how to cook, clean, sew, and look after younger brothers and sisters. Rich boys went to live away from their families at a boarding school. Rich girls were taught at home.

In 1870, **Parliament** agreed there should be a school in every town and village. Still, many children had to work, to help feed the family. By 1880, all children aged five to ten had go to primary school. School teachers wrote down what happened each week. In 1891, teachers wrote: "No fees charged this week". A new law had made primary schools free for all children.

School rules
These rules are from a Sussex school in 1875:
"All children are expected to come to school clean, tidy, and simply dressed. Rough behaviour, fighting, throwing stones or using bad language are strictly forbidden."

What do these rules and photograph tell us about Victorian school life?

By the end of the Victorian age, almost all children went to primary schools, like this one.

In class, children wrote on **slates**, that were wiped clean by spitting and rubbing. For writing on paper, children used a wooden pen with a sharp metal nib, dipped into an ink well (a small pot containing ink). Naughty boys were beaten with a cane (bendy rod), and other punishments included being made to stand in the corner or write lines – such as "I must be truthful" – 100 times or more. PE or drill meant a lot of marching and arm-swinging, but children were taught to sing and play games as well.

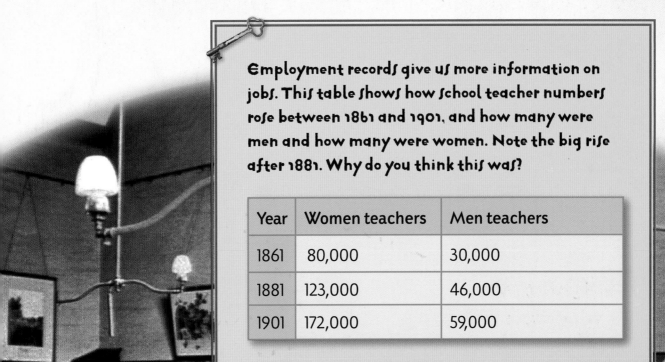

Employment records give us more information on jobs. This table shows how school teacher numbers rose between 1861 and 1901, and how many were men and how many were women. Note the big rise after 1881. Why do you think this was?

Year	Women teachers	Men teachers
1861	80,000	30,000
1881	123,000	46,000
1901	172,000	59,000

Women at work

Poor women had to work at home, doing sewing, for example. Many also did hard, physical jobs – sorting coal, working in factories, and cleaning as servants. Better-off women stayed at home. In the 1851 **census**, the term "housewife" was used for the first time, to describe a woman who ran a home for her husband and children.

6.00 a.m. Get up, clean fireplaces. Carry jugs of hot water (for washing) to family and guests' rooms

8.00 a.m. Breakfast in the Servants' Hall (staff dining room)

8.30 a.m. to 1.30 p.m. Clean, make beds, carry coal buckets upstairs, and empty "slops" (chamber pots)

1.30 p.m. Lunch

2.00 to 8.00 p.m. Dust, sweep, clean glass and china. Light bedroom fires, light candles and oil lamps before it gets dark

8.00 p.m. Supper, while family and guests have dinner. Tidy bedrooms, check bedroom fires

11.00 p.m. Take bedtime drinks to guests

11.30 p.m. Go to bed, tired out.

Diaries kept by servants in big houses tell us how hard they worked. The schedule above is based on the diary of a servant at Tatton Park in Cheshire. A maid was paid between £1 and £2 a month.

◀ This painting shows a housemaid ironing. She would heat the iron on the stove, and use a cloth to hold the hot handle.

Leading the way

Elizabeth Garrett Anderson (1836–1917) was the first woman doctor in Britain. Her sister Millicent Garrett Fawcett (1847–1929) argued for women's right to vote. Their friend Emily Davies (1830–1921) started a college for women students, now part of Cambridge University.

As more schools for girls were started, the first women students went to university. Women took new jobs, as doctors and teachers. Others worked in offices, using new technology, such as typewriters (from the 1870s) and telephones (from the 1880s).

Most women – though not all – wanted the right to vote, and the same pay as men doing the same job. Some men agreed this was fair, but others thought women should stay at home. This was the start of the **suffragette** movement. It was 1918 before women got the right to vote.

Holidays and fun

At home, Victorians played games or sang songs around the piano. Poor people sang or danced to the music of a "fiddle" (violin), a tin whistle, or a street musician playing an instrument called a barrel organ. Everyone enjoyed fireside stories and jokes – especially at Christmas. Christmas crackers were a Victorian invention.

Before the 1800s only rich people had holidays, but the railways brought cheap travel to all. City workers went off to the seaside, to enjoy the sand, donkey rides, and Punch and Judy shows. In the summer, many factories and **textile mills** shut down for a week or two, so machines could be cleaned or mended. These "Wakes Weeks" became workers' holidays. There were also Bank Holidays, when banks shut, and most workers had the day off. On May Day (1st May) there were street processions and dancing around a tall wooden pole with ribbons on it, called a maypole.

▼ This photograph shows people having fun at the seaside. Notice that these children kept most of their clothes on!

The things the Victorians started:

- Christmas cards, first sent in the 1840s
- Fish and chip shops, from the 1860s
- Bank Holidays, started in 1871
- The Christmas pantomime, with celebrity stars from the 1880s.

Town children played in the streets. Rich children played at home, or in the garden. Sport became very popular, and the rules of many modern sports we play (such as badminton and tennis) were made up by the Victorians.

Fun fact

At country fairs, people could win a pig – but they had to catch it first, and the pig was covered in slippery soap!

▲ These Victorian women are playing tennis in a garden.

Victorian sporting firsts

1829 Oxford v Cambridge Boat Race
1839 Grand Liverpool Steeplechase (Grand National) horse race
1869 Britain's first cycle-racing track built
1871 First rugby international
1872 First FA Cup Final
1875 Snooker first played by British soldiers in India
1875 First cross-Channel swim
1876 Indoor ice skating (London)
1877 England play cricket against Australia
1877 Wimbledon tennis championship
1885 Cresta Run (toboggan) started
1896 Modern Olympic Games first held in Athens

Many of our sports started in Victorian times, as this timeline shows.

New ideas

Some of the many inventions and discoveries that changed life for Victorian children are shown on the timeline opposite. At school, children followed on a map the travels of explorers such as David Livingstone, who went across Africa. Lucky children also saw amazing inventions at the **Great Exhibition** of 1851. Thomas Cook ran tours to London for the exhibition, which attracted millions of visitors.

▼ This picture from 1851 shows visitors looking around the Great Exhibition.

Fun fact

At the entrance to the Great Exhibition was a giant lump of coal. It weighed 24 tonnes!

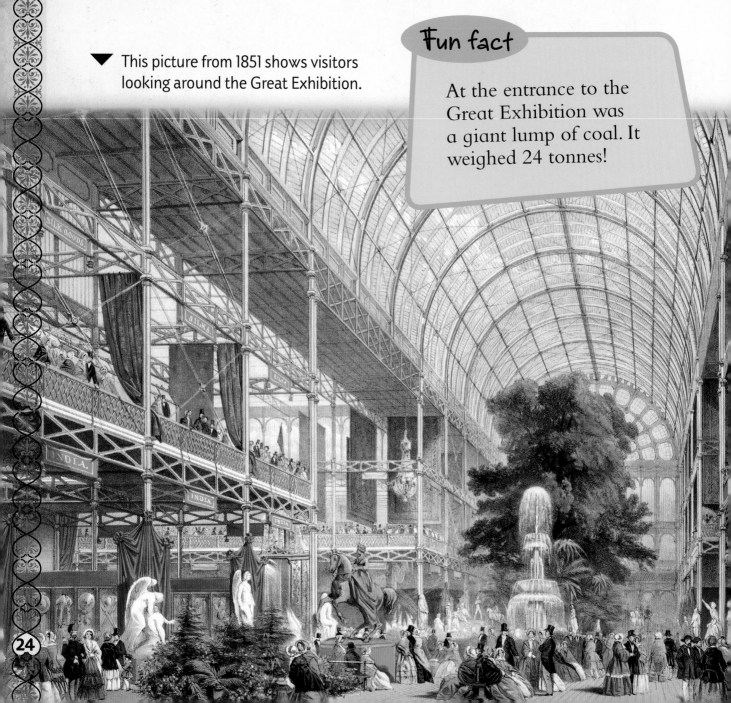

In the 1850s, naturalist Charles Darwin put forward his idea about how living things had evolved (changed) over millions of years. Most people in Britain were Christians. They were taught the Bible story that God made the world and everything in it. Darwin's new idea caused a lot of arguments.

Other new ideas caught on without argument. Photography was a big hit. People could also listen to music on a squeaky record or watch a jerky film. Children had new toys, too – clockwork trains and boats, talking dolls with real hair, and model **steam engines**. They read books written specially for children, such as *Black Beauty* and *Treasure Island*, and cheap comics, such as the *Halfpenny Marvel*.

A Victorian genius

Isambard Kingdom Brunel (1806–59) was a brilliant engineer. He helped his father build the first tunnel beneath the River Thames in London. Brunel went on to build the Great Western Railway, and three famous steamships – *Great Western* (1837), *Great Britain* (1843), and *Great Eastern* (1858). Each was the biggest ship in the world in its day.

Victorian inventions

1807	Steam ship	**1879**	Electric light
1830	Train	**1879**	Electric train
1839	Pedal bicycle	**1880s**	Flush toilet with pull-chain
1840s	Anaesthetics (pain-killers) for operations	**1884**	Fountain pen
1865	Antiseptics (germ-killers)	**1885**	Car
1873	Typewriter	**1890s**	Breakfast cereals
1876	Telephone	**1893**	Zip fastener
1877	Sound recording		

You can see on this timeline that many key inventions were thought up in Victorian times.

The British Empire

Despite so much progress, many children still lived very hard lives. In 1865, the preacher William Booth was shocked to see poor women giving beer to tiny babies. He went on to found the Salvation Army in 1878. Thomas Barnardo found hundreds of poor children sleeping rough in London's back streets, with no one to care for them. He started his first home for boys in 1870.

Every schoolchild knew about the **British Empire**. On the map, the British bits were coloured red. Many people decided to look for a better future by emigrating (moving from one country to settle in another) to Australia, Canada, New Zealand, or South Africa. Others went to the United States. This was not part of the Empire, but in the 1800s it was the "new world" for millions of people from Europe.

▼ These people are waiting to board a ship in Liverpool to emigrate to the United States.

Thousands of British people worked overseas as soldiers, teachers, engineers, traders, or government officials. These "empire-builders" worked in **colonies** in the Caribbean, Africa, and Asia. The Royal Navy steamed the seas to protect trade and keep the peace – which included chasing pirates and slave-traders.

This chart compares the land areas (green bars) and populations (red bars) of the main world powers during the Victorian age. It shows the British Empire was the biggest in population and land area. By 1900, it included about a quarter of the world's people.

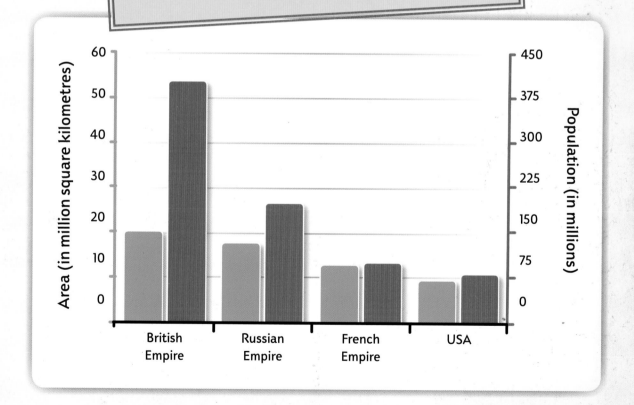

Information explosion

The Victorians lived through a revolution in what we call information technology (IT). They sent messages by **electric telegraph** and telephone, took photographs, and made the first films. New machines printed more newspapers and books. These included stories, such as those by Charles Dickens, and books full of facts, such as schoolbooks, reports from **reformers**, the government, school boards, and sports clubs. All kinds of people, from servants to the queen herself, kept diaries and wrote letters.

An important source of information is the **census**, first carried out in 1801 and held every 10 years since. By 1841, the census asked everyone what job they did. From 1871, it asked their full names, and by 1901, it asked who used which rooms in a house.

▲ This photograph shows Queen Victoria's funeral procession passing through London in 1901.

You can find out about your local Victorian history at the public library, which has copies of old newspapers as well as books. You can also explore Victorian times on the Internet. Try to judge what you see. For example, is a report about a **mine** accident in the words of a miner, a newspaper reporter, or a modern person? Each may have a different point of view. That's history!

Timeline

1819   Queen Victoria is born

1830   Liverpool and Manchester Railway opens

1836   Charles Darwin returns home after a five-year voyage of research

1837   Victoria becomes queen

1839   William Henry Fox Talbot prints the first photograph on paper

1840   First postage stamps, known as "Penny Blacks", go on sale

1842   **Parliament** stops women and children under 10 from working underground in coal **mines**

1847   The 10-hour Act limits working hours for women and children under the age of 18 in factories

1848   The Public Health Act leads to the building of drains and sewers

1851   The **Great Exhibition** opens in London

1860   Brunel's giant ship *Great Eastern* sails across the Atlantic

1861   Victoria's husband, Prince Albert, dies

1863   London's first underground railway, the Metropolitan Line, is built

1876   Alexander Graham Bell invents the telephone in the United States

1877   Thomas Edison's "phonograph" is the first sound recording machine in the United States

1879   The first electric light bulb is invented separately by Edison in the United States and Joseph Swan in Britain

1885   The first motor car is built in Germany by Karl Benz

1888   Cheap box cameras for taking "snapshots" go on sale

1891   All children receive free education until the age of 12

1896   London's first public screening of a film

1899   The Boer War begins in South Africa

1901   Queen Victoria dies

Glossary

average number found by adding amounts together and dividing the total by the number of amounts. The average of 2, 4, and 6 is 4.

British Empire countries ruled by or linked to Britain

census population count to collect information about people

chamber pot Victorian "potty"

colony territory settled by people from another country

electric telegraph system for sending messages along wires

energy in science, this means the force a machine needs to do useful work, such as electricity

evidence picture, writing, an object, or someone's account that tells us what things were like at a particular time

Great Exhibition exhibition of arts and sciences, which was held in London in 1851

harvest time season for gathering crops on a farm

Industrial Revolution changes in manufacturing that started in the 1700s, with the first factory machines

lodging house very cheap hotel, where poor people could spend the night

mine place where coal, iron, or other materials are dug from the ground

Parliament group of people who make the laws of a country

reformer person who tries to change something to improve it

slate shiny, grey-black rock that splits easily into thin sheets. It was used for writing on.

slum poor area with bad housing, dirt, and disease

steam engine machine that heats water to make steam, and uses the steam to drive machinery

suburb area where people live that is a short distance from the centre of a town

suffragette campaigner for women's right to vote

tenement tall building with small rooms, each with a family living in it

textile mill factory for spinning wool or cotton, and weaving them into cloth

workhouse hostel for the poor and jobless, where residents were fed in return for work

Find out more

Books

Children in History: Victorians, Kate Jackson Bedford (Franklin Watts, 2009)

Life in the Past: Victorian Britain, Mandy Ross (Heinemann Library, 2006)

Victorian Britain: Victorian Industry and Science, Neil Tonge (Franklin Watts, 2009)

A Victorian Childhood: At Work, Ruth Thomson (Franklin Watts, 2007)

Websites

This BBC website contains detailed insights into Victorian children's school, work, and play:

http://www.bbc.co.uk/schools/victorians/

You can find lots of information about Victorian life at:
http://www.learningcurve.gov.uk/victorianbritain/default.htm

Places to visit

Museum of Childhood
42 High Street
Royal Mile
Edinburgh EH1 1TG

National Railway Museum
Leeman Road
York YO26 4XJ
www.nrm.org.uk

V&A Museum of Childhood
Cambridge Heath Road
London E2 9PA
http://www.vam.ac.uk/moc/

Index